A LIFE WITHOUT MONEY
and other poems

PERRY BRASS

Belhue Press

Copyright, 2024 © by Perry Brass

Published in the United States of America by:

Belhue Press
2501 Palisade Avenue, Suite A1
Bronx, NY 10463

Electronic mail address: belhuepress@earthlink.net

ALL RIGHTS RESERVED: No part of this book may be reproduced in any form without written permission from the author, except for brief passages for review purposes in a newspaper or magazine. This book is a complete book of fiction. Any resemblance to living persons is coincidental and unintentional.

Cover and interior design by Tom Saettel.
Cover image by Jack Balas
ISBN (10): 1-892149-38-9
ISBN: (13): 978-1-892149-38-1

Cover image by Jack Balas, 2023; THE ACT OF GOD (detail)
Oil & enamel on canvas, 32x48 inches
Image courtesy of the artist and CLAMP, New York
www.Clampart.com
www.JackBalas.com

ACKNOWLEDGEMENTS

There are so many people I'd like to acknowledge here, most especially Hugh Young, Ricardo Limon, the wonderful poet Walter Holland who was so helpful in organizing this book, my fellow coordinators at the Rainbow Book Fair, Sarah Chinn, Darrell Perry, and Daniel Kitchen; and of course all those people over the years who have loved and encouraged my work. Also Tom Saettel, and my friends Jim Marks, Felice Picano, Lee Ellis, Mary Anne Gray, Marnie Wood, Susan Iadone, John Ollom, Jack Balas, Bill Crist, Gary DePasquale, Jim Teschner, Alex Mustelier, John Finch, Steven Dansky, Martha Shelley, Mark Horn, Mark Segal, Ellen Broidy, John Knoebel, Flavia Rando, Dajenya Shoshanna Kafele, Barry Phillips, Richard Sime, and Linda Manning. I also have to acknowledge so many people who are no longer physically here, but whose presence I feel so much: Jeffrey Lann Campbell, Tom Finley, Chris DeBlasio, Michael Dash, among so many others taken from us too early, as well as Mimi Stern-Wolfe who adored my poetry and its relationship to music.

OTHER BOOKS BY PERRY BRASS:

Sex-charge (poetry)

Mirage, a science fiction novel

Works and Other 'Smoky George' Stories

Circles, the sequel to *Mirage*

Out There: Stories of Private Desires. Horror. And the Afterlife.

Albert or The Book of Man, the third book in the Mirage series

Works and Other 'Smoky George' Stories, Expanded Edition

The Harvest, a "science/politico" novel

The Lover of My Soul, A Search for Ecstasy and Wisdom (poetry and other collected writings)

How to Survive Your Own Gay Life, An Adult Guide to Love, Sex, and Relationships

Angel Lust, An Erotic Novel of Time Travel

Warlock, A Novel of Possession

The Substance of God, A Spiritual Thriller

The Manly Art of Seduction, How to Meet, Talk to, and Become Intimate with Anyone

King of Angels, A Novel About the Genesis of Identity and Belief

Carnal Sacraments, A Historical Novel of the Future, Set in the Last Quarter of the 21st Century, 2nd Edition

The Manly Pursuit of Desire and Love, Your Guide to Life, Happiness, and Emotional and Sexual Fulfillment in a Closed-Down World

Trial by Night, Two Novellas of Gay Love, Innocence, Horror, and Deception

TABLE OF CONTENTS

A LIFE WITHOUT MONEY   1

NEW YORK IS FULL OF A MILLION PICTURES   6

LET ME BE GRATEFUL   7

THE LORD OF LOST THINGS   8

FOR THE RODRIGUEZ TWINS   9

CNIDARIAN   10

THE LORD OF THE LONELY   11

ENLIGHTENMENT: MARCH 22, 1999   12

INFINITE STARLIGHT   13

FOR TWO TEENAGE BOYS HANGED IN IRAN
   FOR HOMOSEXUAL OFFENSES   14

THE SOUL MATE   15

THE DEATH OF THE PEONIES   16

OK, SO I MET JAMES FRANCO   18

FOUR POEMS FROM FRANCE, AUGUST, 1999
   ALONG THE CANAL IN BURGUNDY   19
   AN ECLIPSE IN EUROPE, AUGUST 11, 1999   20
   AT ORNANS, THE FAMOUS   21
   I CAN NOT BELIEVE IT   22

A LULLABY FOR THE EARTH   24

FOUR POEMS FROM COSTA RICA
   COSTA RICA   25
   TRUMPET FLOWERS   26
   THE MOVIE OF MY MIND   27
   MIDNIGHT IN BARÚ   29

THE "FOUR LAST SONGS" AT IKEA   29

DEATH AWAKENING   01

VISAGES   31

THE ISLAND OF BOYHOOD   32

THE TRAIN EMERGES   33

MASERATI   34

A EULOGY FOR BERNARD MADOFF   35

IMMETTE ST. GUILLAN   36

CLIFTON WEBB   37

I WILL ASK MIKE PENCE TO KISS ME   38

STILL IN LOVE WITH LANCE ARMSTRONG   39

O'SHEA   40

THE FORGOTTEN CHILDREN   41

THE RESTLESS YEARNING TOWARDS MY SELF   42

SEVEN P.M. IN SAN FRANCISCO   44

TWA FLIGHT 800   45

ALL SELFIES, ALL THE TIME?   46

A WALK THROUGH OLD UDAIPUR   47

CUBA IN THE MORNING   48

AS YOU LEAVE THE TRAIN   49

NEW YORK IS FILLED WITH BOYS   50

SIR GAWAIN AT CHRISTMAS   51

WHITE CHRISTMAS   53

STARLIGHT AT CANAAN   54

FOR GREG LOUGANIS   55

FOR TWO COPS—FOR JASON RIVERA,
    AND WILBERT MORA, 27   56

FOR JACK NICHOLS, 1938-2005   57

PATRICK KENNEDY LEAVES   58

THE DEATH OF ISAAC   51

FAME   63

FOR EJAY WEISS   62

THE LAST WEDNESDAY IN AUGUST   63

GREG BUCKLEY, JR. 21-YEAR-OLD MARINE LANCE CORPORAL
    MURDERED IN AFGHANISTAN   64

THE STRANGE, SHY MELANCHOLY OF LA ROTONDA   65

THE ANGELS   67

WHAT WE DID NOT KNOW   69

THE TRAIN STATION AT SPUYTEN DUYVIL   70

THE POETS DO NOT SING SONGS ANYMORE   71

NOTES ON THE POEMS

ABOUT PERRY BRASS

OTHER BOOKS BY PERRY BRASS

FOREWORD

This is my first book of poetry in a long time, since *The Lover of My Soul* in 1998. So much has happened since then, although I feel that the basic calling and landscape of my work has not changed, that is, to tell the truth and still hold close to the beauty, rigor, joy, sound, and feeling of language. As a poet, I have been extremely fortunate that a lot of people have loved and enjoyed my work, certainly enough to set a great number—over a hundred—of my poems to music. I am an unabashedly lyrical poet; I love the sound and texture of English, and the inner structural music of poetry. Some poets want to stay as far away from that as possible, and that is their prerogative, but I really love it when the words start doing somersaults in the air, and sneak into your brain and stay there.

I have noticed that a number of these poems are about leave-taking, and remembering people who have passed on. That makes sense for someone my age who has been writing for more than fifty years. But I also recognize and write about the lives and traumas of children and younger people, too. It has never been easy to be young, but being young now is especially difficult, and I can see that and feel it in my work. When I tell people that the name of my book is *A Life Without Money*, they really snap up to it. "Yes, I understand that a lot," they say. In the Age of Donald Trump, money has meant a punishing everything. That may be a part of life in America, but it seems to be even more so now.

These are very urban poems, because I have lived most of my life in New York City. Sometimes they reflect other urban poets like Frank O'Hara or Edward Field, writers who celebrated the marvel of New York life as it reached them in good and bad times. They are also very much "gay" poems in the not-so-old meaning of gay, that is, they are poems that speak openly of same-sex desire and love, but in doing so also embrace any kind of love, its rewards and difficulties. So I hope you don't have to be "gay-ish" (to borrow some terminology from George Santos) to read these poems, but—it doesn't hurt either if you are.

I also wanted to include poems of real quotidian life, poems to my barber, to my super who retired, to regular things that are lost, and personal things that are found, like a soul mate. There are poems to people I have never met, like Mike Pence and James Franco, part of the environment of politics and celebrity we are all mired in. The truth is, although a lot of people are now unfortunately afraid of reading poetry—they feel they just don't "get" it—poetry itself should not be afraid of anything, even in our very divided times.

So I hope that readers of this collection will have that feeling of no fear, of the joy poetry exposes us to, and even some deeper wistfulness. Because the truth is, you are sharing these poems with me now, too.

Perry Brass

A LIFE WITHOUT MONEY

You're alive and every pore of you
is open to those possibilities, fantastic
calibrations of a world that won't
      end with you, but will go on
in its illusions, while you watch amazed,
      beguiled as a four year old
learning to attach signs to meaning,
but of you—what can you attach to make
your own yearnings succeed in the wreck
of reality—you now in this elixir of euphoria
arising in its adrenalized fury to the very edge
of hysteria—how could you help it, and why?

      Picasso ate ruthlessly and painted
with his teeth, pecker, and scrotum—
    so it occurred to you. *You?*
          You—
who were you in this maelstrom,
in this sack of your own engorged self?
The artist within you rebelled and the wizard smirked.
Neither had answers, while the vulgar monster
that you hid in your own ambitions, clothed in clichés
accepted by half-wits, the thing that educated you
from its own plight and window-show of experience,
        told you: accept no consequences
other than how you can bend shiny circumstance.

Accept this as a prayer, a thing clerical and magical,
a work of art that you can climb into and constitute
with your own clandestine acts, refingered now
like a Bach cantata on the grounds of renewable religion.

How do you do it—and live? Murder would be complicated
and messy, and the energy you'd need to take anything
      would never exceed the gain.
You did a little study, a flow chart, an imbecilic
squandering practical as a traffic ticket,
and all that you arrived at was—staying alive

menaces you, despite your own dumb delight
        which presently defines you: too
pretty to excuse away, it's too lovely to let wither,
and you're sad that it might deflate like a soufflé
when your own heat has been siphoned
by the jokes and dicks of working stiffs: Ah!
The confounded truth: wars are exactly waged
                for this,
to keep jerks like you engaged and stoking
in a scheme that makes no sense, has no outcome,
but keeps you fed, clothed, and silly with
        its own stupifications. Ah, adventure!
        And the swindle that calls itself
by so many names: "simple" morality;
a "life plan" nailed to your numbered bank account;
and "tunnel vision," remember that?
They threw you in a pit and packed the opening with dirt—
you were reminded you needed it: only look at the good,
    the big win, a perfect society washed clean
of homeless unreliables—that swindle!—you worked with it,
                      ate it, lived on it

                    while life,
more enchanting than any gilt-edged bubble
eluded you. It was not in your tunnel, what they
dug for you. You were deceived, mutilated and let go
        with a flow of Christian sympathy:
all crap and phony—sure, you knew it, but stayed
too deep in your hole yet to show it.

Or know it.

Till you burrowed out, all bile and craziness—
with nothing left to lose except some last
illusion of erectile perfection. And that stank
as you sank into penury.   But a distant light
straight from the A-hole of darkness faced you—
It blinked neon pink and white: Starvation
              like a tape worm
                would eat you,

unless you learned to lie with the best of them,
reclining among the liars, groping to snip
their own grapes. The twits at work
who on occasion only claimed their own traces
in the john, flushing down daily with the shit
their own starry selves   the self
they dodged at night, winking back at them
from their own dark dreams. Flush! Gone!
            You thought
about running drugs or marrying for money—
who doesn't?   But both by definition

devour the truth of you, only leaving for evidence
some silky membrane left from your own smile. So

you chose to be a mercenary in a mercenary time
and got away with it, until the eyes of the kids who died
                        on the streets in sad fury

        soaked you in such anguish
that your stomach turned raw from heaving
and your nuts shriveled from revulsion. You
were an outcast again. You'd blown your own in-
dependence, bought at the price of servitude.

But—so many men who go in for ideals only end up
        in self-inflicted cruelty: you knew it. You were smart
enough to see it, in that same path of virtue that
had brought you on this course: the one where you
could touch yourself and claim your own tender soul.
                      Shithead!
You'd put to sword your own hunger then fed it
with monstrosities, still any decent developer
has a better story. Count on that. So you were left

with piddling alternatives: drop out in a commune,
make tofu ice cream for tourists in Kansas,
become a Jesus-dope or a monk bled by his own
perversions of sensuality: pain, deprivation, prayer.
                      You

                                        knew
                                          it,
you could do it, if you had to—to preserve that
little piece of you you'd allow no one else to buy—
lucky you! You believed in "authenticity"
before it got offered on the Shopping Network
or the girly yoga catalogs sent out weekly
from marketers in Reno. You had it: you could see it,
this little face of yours with the bird wings
attached and the eyes blue as oranges, blue
as honey from the deepest ocean, and you

                              didn't want it

to leave you, no matter what the cost or penalty.
You would have to lie to the liars and outpriest
the priests, you'd have to be ruthless to drop
defenses like *trou*—if only to yourself. How lonely
                 it was, rotten as that delicious
narcissism of responsibility choking you, stuffing
itself with your own marrow and shitting out
                       your daily sorrow.

Finally, you decided—trippy, giddy, renewed
by your own charm—to join the happy throngs,
witless as they were but enjoying their own
business, gleeful as the Bronx fans after a shut-out
Yankees game—wherever there is religion
                    in the daily seeking of oblivion,
you went for it. You tilted yourself upside down
to do it, burrowing deep into your own weakness.
                       It was so safe.
Sleep without death. Just do it! A degree
of Christian charity like a cigarette before
a firing squad or a loan against a gambling debt—
so: you will not drown. You went on like this,
a blind traveler speaking only to the blind.

You decided to renounce money, become ascetic,
live on the beach. Like a bleached surfer dude.
You parked cars, cleaned houses, stole lawn stuff
from the rich and tithed to the poor, to gutter
guys who knew a lot but sadly not it all. You

studied God and saw nothing good in it,
except the same blind alleys. But one day

                       on the beach
I got enlightened as a storm came in
swelling the air until it broke upon me
like a fever, pouring rain
                       as beneficence
             upon my skin.
    I smiled. Life is short. We are blessed with it
but most are too poor to know this. They run after
everything including the fatalities of destiny.
They are bereft of love and bankrupt of all
human richness. They spend zillions on the blind
pursuits of art instead of the living pursuits
of experience—of seeing and being.
Love was as merciless as hate, but more pleasant
to curl within its clutches. This I learned. This
was a life without money.

NEW YORK IS FULL OF A MILLION PICTURES

New York is full of a million pictures,
and they can all be boiled down to this:
the person who knows his own mind
and is looking for a short cut to it,
the person who has hidden her spirit
under clothes she cannot afford,
the person who is completely fulfilled
and feels inadequate because of it,
the person whose job it is to see inside you
                                      for a split second
and to reward you with this knowledge;
the person of the streets, the person of the
                                                  parks,
and the person of the dawn sky renewing
himself with every year and every movement
of the city's great river, spilling its banks
                            to find a novel course
inside the brain of night.

LET ME BE GRATEFUL

Let me be grateful for my existence,
for this journey, for this story
I've been called to tell; for this role
I've pulled over my head like
a hood, or a shirt to fool
            the world against
my stark innocence, against
a nakedness too painful
to reveal. Let me be grateful,
not humble, but grateful,
and let me arm myself
with gratitude and submit it
as a gift to the great forces
that have left me here, beached
like Ulysses on a distant shore,
far away from my beginning,
but grateful for all this world
that meets my eyes.

THE LORD OF LOST THINGS

Lost keys and lost youth
and lost time; lost time
and lost looks and lost hope.
Lost opportunities and moments
when the wind blew away fragments
of joy, of yesterday in your pocket
and today in your heart.
                        Of truth
lost and truth squandered in
convenient denial; of lost thoughts
and pennies tossed into the face
of prosperity that frowned. The great

Lord of Lost Things collects them and
places them in a world of our own
                                dreaming
where the angels gather them in small
                                wicker baskets
as food for the soul, when it awakens.

FOR THE RODRIGUEZ TWINS

You are angels—you have to be,
somewhere above or among us,
protecting us with your sweet
and quiet gaze, your infant seriousness,
your enchanting ability to step into
        that neutral space beyond loss,
                  forgetfulness,
oblivion and tragedy. You will
protect us, all of us, most especially
your father wounded by weakness
                and frailty,
called upon for explanations
that he cannot conjure from despair.
You are so small. You are impossible
to hold, your tiny hands, your feet,

your faces with eyes that now
see everything, everything
that cannot be named, or called
forth into the future, that cannot
                  know
the noise and bother, the sweet
smell of pudding, the bitter smell
of circumstance, of defeat.
All will be over. All will be
grass and blue moonlight
and the living will stop crying
your names, little guys.
But you will know them. You
will know your names. Always.

One-year-old Luna and Phoenix Rodriguez die in August in the backseat of a car after being left in a parking lot by their father who was at work.

CNIDARIAN

All speckled with light
and jelly and silvered flecks of salt,
all twisting and gliding
and catching drools
of amber before they fall
into grist along the sand: it shoots
a spew of water and wriggles forward,
menacing, floating close. Who says
beauty is simple? Complicate me,
detain me. Make me afraid; I will gasp
to catch my breath, then bloat
with air to come up, to become one
with your layer beneath the waves,
where sunlight is refracted
in my observant pulse, where any dream
                is lethal until the night
sucks the tide through its course.

THE LORD OF THE LONELY

How I will give myself
to you, how I will offer
you true lingering solace,
the immeasurable kingdom,
the short balm of hope and
      the long balm
           of decent love,

of the great world viewed
as good and not bad. Of the idea
of yourself as good, as God,
as love waiting, as love offered,
as love found at the end
          of your journey,
aside from the normal business,
aside from the nine-to-five,
aside from every formality,
except for honor, naked,
        splendid,
    giving you
the promise you want.

ENLIGHTENMENT: MARCH 22, 1999

I am enlightened: all at once.
Walking across Forty-Third Street
from Grand Central to Broadway,
in the low, graceful, dying light
of evening, I realize
that every human being
has a singular consciousness
inside, and that men only want
to release the "bird," the woman,
inside them; as women
want to find the tree: "their man."
But some men are the bird
and some women are the tree.
And so we know this.

I find myself slowing down
to the point of death. While
the calm inside me seeps out
to spread its glow
on the pitted sidewalks
and the walls and the people
around me. And this is all
there really is now; this is
the bones and the matter inside.
This is what death is,
embracing, fearless, finally
watching the world fade from me,
inside my own silence.
A silence not lonely.
Without tears.

INFINITE STARLIGHT

Soon it'll be over. Before
we know it. Before anyone can
judge it, before the fear and
the rapture of forgiveness
is gone—when we hold on
to that last point of light
seeping through the gloom,
bringing us such pleasure
such exquisite lifting,
up, up toward that momentary

threshold where art dances
to the distant music of
                eternity
that only art can hear. That
distant mermaid's song
like the sea whispering not
to the drowning but to
                the saved.
And that's when we see it,
that infinite starlight,
cold, cold as metal; warm as
the dying light of love.

FOR TWO TEENAGE BOYS HANGED IN IRAN FOR HOMOSEXUAL OFFENSES

You were murdered by the followers
of a god who would not harm you;
like all the spiteful, two-bit marshals
of the holy spirit, your hang men will not
suffer for your deaths: only I will,
and all people of kind will, of honest
feelings laid bare by sadness. You were
kids; you should have been playing video
games and fooling around in the back seats
at drive-in movies or beaches, or places
where the hormonal tides wash in
on shy curiosities approached by temptation.
Such ventures are not to be punished
as harshly as sixteenth century treason,
but the worst monsters are the righteous,
the defamers of nature, who know so little
and preach so loud. I will offer
a sanctification for you, a cigarette
of incense, some honey cake soaked
in tears and the sky.

THE SOUL MATE

You will find him at the
end of the movie, or the beginning
of the second act, that embraceable
substance, that discovery like
antique apples or bespoke chocolate
        that you never understood,
and now he's here, and you
are crying from the bottom
of your stomach, tears rise.
The mystery has been solved
and its simplicity is destroying
you—you were so hardheaded,
so matter-of-fact, and now
the fact is here. You can't explain
it to your friends who wink suddenly,
and smirk, and give you useless
advice: but it—*he*—is here,
and sunlight is all over you.

THE DEATH OF THE PEONIES

At first they are nothing.
A stubble on the earth
and then their stems shoot up
and tangle and gossip with one another,
and twist their leaves about each other
rancorously, grabbing towards the light
thrusting their fingers out in fisted buds
and penis heads, tight, furled, foreskinned out,
and you wait,
anxiously, hesitantly
for a soaking rain to please them, but not
beat them down. And you dream

about their flesh, their baby whiteness
and rich Latin reds and extravagant nights of them—

drifting out to the garden to smell—
then they burst, and you're shell-
shocked from them: their dazzling, belly-
filling, ruthless gaudiness. Your heart triple
beats around them, a bolero entangled in
          cockatiel plumage, a bed
washed with petals and you're diving in them,
dripping; swimming; sinking obscenely,

licking them—with that scent of apple
          and mango and citrus breeze
and the clean creases of babies and a ripened banana
and rain pounding your throat.
And at night you can't sleep from the thought
that this exalted gallop,
hard, rushing, punching the air—
its moments are numbered. You must go
out and kneel in it, as you once made love
to whale sounds on a boat—insane,
but who could control it?
They go off. Your beloved flowers will forget you
and take new partners, while you
can only watch—but this does not stop you
from rolling in the agony—how unseemly, dreamlike,
yet revolting. They have just taken your heart
and popped it and are eating it,
these awkward, hushed blooms turbaned
in the mating call of earth and testicles;

and you blame them. They made you ashamed.
Stripped you. Reached inside and ripped
some vital piece from you, while you
only wanted to lie face down, drenched in their odor,
    in the crotch of their enduring artlessness

as that scent, intimate, fleeting
suddenly clears through you
and you draw up to your knees
and roll into yourself to at last
dissolve what figures between you.
And in a burst, it reaches you:
your own waking nightmare has taken you out
as its victim and pushed its jagged knife
into your chest as the sun beat down,
while you screamed with a gag in your mouth—
*God-take-me-now, God-take-me-now,
now, now—owwww*—till your blood rushed up
and was met by a heaven of simple lips,
    as the Holy Child, knowing, floating
on a cloud of petals blessed you
and kissed that place in your heart
that bled.

    Then all folded into One
rolled into its own thrilling head,
presented on its stem, perfect
through infinity, where its blossom
holds and tempts you
with an aroma of such intensity
that it made you stay alone
in the garden all night.

And in a week or so,
there before you
is that final retreat
when the air takes their petals and drops them
to your feet. And you watch them, exhausted,
mute, stunned, left . . . left in the waiting room
of a choking, single breath.

June 3, 1999
Bronx, New York
For Hugh on his birthday, June 30, 1999

OK, SO I MET JAMES FRANCO

OK, so I met James Franco
at Yale, and I was forty years
younger—only 23—and he bumped
                              into me
on purpose because I was so attractive
and magnetic and alive that he couldn't
ignore me under his Hollywood shades
and hoodie and pretend
that he was disappearing
into regular graduate studenthood,
and we went back to his "rooms"

and made love to Berlioz on his sound system
because he wanted to impress me—
                              a bit,
and himself too, and afterwards
he explained to me that he would love
to walk holding hands with me
                              through the Quads,
but it would be on Facebook in a minute,
and he was captured by his ambition,
a pawn of his history, extradited
to the land of the Famous trying
to be normal while selling their souls
to Mammon, and I smiled. And he smiled back,
with his gentle radiance that could not be
                              captured
or extradited, or released to anyone
except to me, at that moment, in that clear
window of words that we both used
to see each other with.

Note: James Franco is (or was) a graduate student in English at Yale.
Extra note: I have never met him.

FOUR POEMS FROM FRANCE, AUGUST, 1999

ALONG THE CANAL IN BURGUNDY

We went out to a field in France
at night, after a rain had washed
the skies. And they were pierced
with stars and the distant cries
of frogs and children and dogs

and the whispers of history
in the wandering lanes of houses further on,
with their gardens and neat lawns,
and I felt content to know all this
and let it reach me, the way
                France does,
in that off-hand way that doesn't welcome you,
       but tolerates your presence
like a friend who doesn't need to explain
                              anything.
Then I walked back through the gray streets
in a quiet village along a canal in Burgundy,

in Franche-Comtè, what they call the "county,"
because for centuries counts had ruled here
mercilessly, and made the people stony and stubborn
and unexplainable in a certain way
that always hid from explanations.
So I walked back to the boat where I stayed
           on that peaceful canal in Burgundy,
and left the stars outside in France.

Ranchot

AN ECLIPSE IN EUROPE, AUGUST 11, 1999

This has nothing to do with us;
I am sure that centuries ago
they burned witches on this ground
when the moon came between
them and good sense: the darkness at noon,
the terrifying cold light; the silence,
the cowering herds of farm animals.
These once foretold Evil,
the *mal occhio*, the coming Fire.

Then quickly it was over
and one had to assemble some sanity
around you: the earth continued
its movement and the Moon passed
        benignly beyond them,
into darkness, into night where the Moon belonged.

They would sing then of saintly deliverance
and the songbirds would resume
their little melodies that today
get lost in urban noise, though
we long for them—wistfully, sometimes.

Now the clouds part and bow to the land
below them. The fields exhale briefly—
all this they have seen before—as the noon movement,
    that unsettling darkness, begins; and it feels
like divine love itself, lowering his lips
upon us, delivering magic—or insanity.

Pray for us now, please,
we ask instinctively.
Remember this time at our passing,
when we close our eyes
and Europe disappears from us
forever. Remember us, please, at this moment.

Osselle

AT ORNANS

At Ornans, "birthplace of Gustave Courbet,"
I walked into a frolic of stately trees,
ancient littles yews with mushrooming crowns,
trimmed like spinning tops
held to the ground,
in front of an old church
beside mute cliffs above the town.

The trees welcomed me
with a gravity of peace,
while I sat away from the kids
who'd gone to look for Courbet.
And that, of course, is the odd thing
about those who pursue art—

that only when you find yourself
do you find it: or refind it
and then at once,
refine yourself.

The trees were rough and simple,
gnarled and twisted, but their stoic
homeliness invited me more
than anything to sit and rest
and see art and some other part
of God out there. And I knew

God was holding the little trees
and Gustave Courbet (and me)
in the field of one immense eye—with all
that artistry and awfulness and depth
                        that evades art.
But which sometimes we see
on an afternoon in France,
where the river Loue
slips down into the valleys
and the old yew trees cling tightly
and do their very slow dance.

Ornan

I CAN NOT BELIEVE IT

I can not believe it—we are leaving
                this impossible
           country—
with its glacial service and *sang froid* manners,
where they leave you alone in the parks,
take their dogs everyplace, and smoke ridiculously.
They speak a language you have to suck
your cheeks in to speak, with ideas you have to
cinch your mind in to use. Like a damn corset—
Like an orbit fluttering around the Sun King.
That energy! Divine, decorative, and so wasteful . . .
but not wasted. No, they don't waste a thing—

And you realize they've put on this show
just for you, but without you ever in mind.
It's like the food, buttery, rich, exquisite—
in realistic amounts. Beyond that, it'll quickly kill you.
But you know you've got to leave.
Get out, or it becomes like a party,
where you stayed too long and they laid out
this sparkling, flattering table for you
only later to present that bill
you cannot pay. All that red wine
from the bottom of the glasses— wow!—has gone
straight to your head. The pretty, curtained room

all in white and blue
is revolving; it's time to vamoose.
Your last franc is gone. They're ripping
the scenery from you—the lanes of chestnut trees,
the formal gardens, the vistas of fountains,
those funny little dogs. They are fanning everything
              before you one last time,
like a smart dealer reshuffling the deck.
You paid too much. You smoked too much.
Your clothes are dirty, and it's almost dawn.
It is time to leave France. *La Gloire* is choking
the breath out of you: that ageless dance of power here
has gathered around you; dismissive and inviting
at once. And frightening. *Oui?*
It's time to leave France before it gets you,
when you find you can't pay anymore,

before it finds you soon too dazed
                    by staying
in this impossible country, where like the wines,
they leach your brain from you and then throw you
something that suddenly—really—humbles you.
They will knock you to your knees with their questions
you can't answer and words you'll never pronounce.
The puff pastry will start to taste like road dust
while the sidewalks become too slick from memories.
Oh, it's time to leave this beguiling country.
          But first, you've got to reach
the right door.

4:30 a.m. Paris.

A LULLABY FOR THE EARTH

Goodnight my sweet thing, O my
charmer of mercies, with eyes as deep
as the closing sky, eyes of blackness
and eyes of gray sorrow, and eyes
as bright as a rainbow's smile.

Let me count ringlets, let me count toes,
let me count valleys where nobody goes;
let me count doorways and weeds by the road,
and quick, drifting isles where the sleepy child roams;
let me count faces awake in the dark, and places
too tired to face morning.

I will bring gladness, hot tea and toast,
warm buttered sandwiches, plump jelly rolls;
let me bring everything I can hide
inside my satchel, forty miles wide.
Inside my fullness, inside my hope,
and inside the harvest of plenty.

I'll make you safe, sweet bode
where I dream. I will bring
copper, fresh paint, and the sun.
I will bring dew for the birds
in the fields, and take all your
great wounds and bid them to rest.

FOUR POEMS FROM COSTA RICA

COSTA RICA

I'm in a land Joseph Conrad dreamed about,
of jungles, monkeys, and eagles,
and vistas out to two seas. My third night out

I got food poisoning, throwing my guts up,
chasing to the toilet, with careening tides of nausea.
It passed and the friendly *ticos* smiled at me:
      The gringo is sick, how sad!

We drove through forests and mountains
bleached in clouds, on roads bumpy
with craters from the moon. Your eyes tire
of the magnificence; your stomach is in your throat.

The monkeys at night make a noise
like distant, slapping thunder; and dogs bark,
always dogs, roaming the countryside
and the towns, bony mongrels who look half-goat.

The air is full of contagious merriment and a past
of Indians and magic that haunts like the dark cloud
in San Jose, sticking to the volcano out my window
whose lingering fire I can feel through the wet.

Feb 15, 2009
Puerto Viejo, Costa Rica

TRUMPET FLOWERS

The fat white, pink-rimmed trumpet flowers
open only at night, and expel
their satiny sweetness

for the large moths and tiny birds
whose tongues and shit
will nourish them.

Feb. 15, 2009
Puerto Viejo, Costa Rica

THE MOVIE OF MY MIND

A young white man with a classical body
is playing badminton on the beach at Puerto Viejo
with a small black boy who volleys back
to him, chasing the birdie up in the air. They

stop while the surf whirls at their toes,
and a family washes the bottom of an infant girl
lifted out of her wet diapers while her grandparents
look on smiling, and birds whistle among the flowers.

It is a frieze flattened by distance, but made
dimensional by my brain. I want to
keep looking, playing the scene
through my eyes. The birds, the languid
dogs, the hissing surf sounds—all recede.

Until there is only the young man
with the classical body, playing badminton
with the little boy . . . then they are gone
       unpreserved, except for words.

Feb 16, 2009
Puerto Viejo, Cost Rica

MIDNIGHT IN BARÚ

Van Gogh's "Starry Night at Saint Remy" has nothing
over midnight in Barú up in the mountains, where the heavens
put on a fireworks show, sending starbursts of brilliance
out from eternity, where the jaguar's eyes smile
in the distance, and sparks of birds and night flowers
shake out jewels into the dewy dark.

If I could just climb up there and dance with you stars,
shake all the dust out of my own being and become
as young as your eternal fire. But I can only look.
Your dance outwits me: its story of gods and warring
constellations is too old and unflinching in its
constant freshness, its life and being, as the stars

pass fire like gas after beans! Oh, give me just
a second of your twirling watchworks
sprinkled with the lights of dreams awake,
then I will sleep the way men have always done,
solid and wordless as insects, seeing only
sequined sorties of light.

Feb 19, 2009, 12:09 a. m.
Los Aguas, a mountain resort in the district of Barú

THE "FOUR LAST SONGS" AT IKEA

I am at Ikea in Red Hook
shopping with Robert when suddenly
the "Four Last Songs" of Richard Strauss
come in on my radio earphones—
this plaintive end of civilization,
of the rich complexity of Europeanism—
here in this vast temple and warehouse
of mass taste, or the "unique," the
                      sadly "unique,"
with the crowd wondering, sizing,
making comparisons, figuring, looking,
not looking; everyone so propelled,
                      wrought invisible by purpose—
The things! The numbers! The savings!
The stuff! The desire to struggle
through such plenitude unkinks
the twisting coils of life, reducing
conflicts with a snap gesture
towards perfectly matching merchandise.
Yippee! Yikes! Found it! Everything
is here! Disappear along the aisles,
and mourn not for any artifact gone:
It's all recyclable, truly. Even tomorrow is.
Even I am. I am incarnate.
                Myself.
I know it. Now,
Right here at Ikea.

DEATH AWAKENING

I died and the only light left
was Ricardo naked but clothed
in shimmering flesh, like
the sky linked with stars, his
hair, lips, and eyes glowing
like New York in the velvet dark;
like the winter night that comes
out of the park to hold me
and speak in quiet truths, and there

he was, large like the sky,
the one thing of life to find me
in death and pull me by

my silent heart
waiting to be returned
to the world again.

VISAGES

The visage of the boy looking
out the window on the train
and I see only his unknowing
reflection, unknowing that I
am seeing him, watching his eyes
take in each yard of the distance
between here and the yet
                unknowable there.
And the visage of autumn
in the last moment of expiring,
leaves on the ground grinding
                to dust,
without art, without words,
without poets, without any goodness
or badness in its face, but the face

will soon turn white in winter.
And the visage of time watching me,
seeing my vanity, my frustrations,
my hope calling forth vainly,
my despair when I miss fortune,
my unknowing despair
when every blessing has been shared
                with me
from stars I cannot even envision,
as they are too great, I know, for
my own meager visage.

THE ISLAND OF BOYHOOD

I left it . . . its time is gone,
a date only making sense
going backwards. There is
the low mist and the open sky,
        the wide smile of a lake
with my swim trunks down; sleep-
away camp; threats of exposure,
        of revelation,
        of not being sure of anything
while siphoning forbidden treats
from the twisted pipes of appetite,
        bare-assed friskiness,
        dreams and sorrow.
And now we can find its map, its contours
in a half-remembered face, features fresh
and so pleasant compared to the damage
they will do later to the fulfillment of desires:
        I will
        leave you,

and go out into a small inlet
hidden almost by trees where the games
you hosted bringing terror to the losers
have ceased, and the stark pain of awakening
has been assuaged by some regret
and then acceptance.

Here is the calm I met
on forgotten beaches, and night
creeping upon me in a cool whisper
delights me with its random noises
and the distant squeals of carnivals
and the dying flash of entertainments.

Long ago I left you
        in an aching shiver,
even with my head spinning
with such accomplishments
that I'll bring back again to you—as a bribe
        for you and your little gatekeepers,
if only you will . . . somehow coolly
        without a nod or snicker,
let me back in.

THE TRAIN EMERGES

The train emerges from the Grand Central tunnel
into Harlem in the autumn darkness,
past the windows of a homeless shelter
with cots lined up like mute witnesses,
then a bar, lit in green and olive,
and the blunt fortresses of housing projects,
then the big, wide avenues, wringing tears
in the rain, and back into grumpy darkness.
Cops get on at 125th Street,
and there is a big interchange of tracks
turning into the Bronx, following the river,
and more lights up to the first stop,
Morris Heights, while inside
the ghost-fatigue of voices talks against
the chug and tug of wheels, the tracks,
and the slip of the world pulling back,
taking you back to the same thing
tomorrow.

MASERATI

You're walking down W. 43rd Street at night
toward Grand Central and there on the sidewalk
sits a white Maserati—sleek, brand new, kissing
the lights with its bloom of a chassis,
        like some red-headed kid's dream
of mastery, desire, escape—a release that speeds
into the ether of showing: encounters with dough
and brain-blank pick-ups on Madison Avenue—
the painless accretion of family bank notes; the discovery
of riches down in South America, with the rush of cocaine
through the eyeballs of sleep. And here

you see *you* in the driver's seat
inside another body lean as the sea—with the speed
        of changes and time in your favor, you
like a stallion stealing races, miles ahead of
the nearest pony—snatching the sharp eyes
of the cold world with barely a wink of your own.

Then it's gone. You can't hold it.
Or know it.   Or own it.
Its lavish, slightly sinister presence
that talks in a language that makes you
throw up, its gleaming white carapace
and Moroccan interior—all sucked
into the greasy backfire of time.

A EULOGY FOR BERNARD MADOFF

You cut such a classy figure, Berny,
looking excellent in a polo, or dinner jacket.
You did everything for your wife,
your kids and inner circle, and placed
decorum and discretion above all else.

No one could accuse you of the grandiloquent
effort, putting on a show without taste
or refinement. You came from a generation
that trimmed excess, would not protest
or leave a mess, and kept its
dirty laundry *incognito* in the laundry
room. You were not the first

to grab the check at the table,
but you knew you could cover it one way
or another and with nothing you did not
feel was yours in a copasetic manner.

You schemed to make the world a better place,
and schemed to hold your own in any
company. Some of our schemes
have a way of playing out extra well,
while others have a way of blowing up
in our faces.   On your death

you'll be met by the great Bookkeeper
in the sky, who will take
everything from you as he does
all of us. You will be humbled
                    and tumbled along
for a while, and see all the numbers floating
across your face, taking away each
pixel of feature from the TV screen,
from the digital iteration of each sin.

You will be left as we all have been,
knowing less and less and less. But
finally finding mercy in our last
                    engagement
on the field of ignorance.

IMMETTE ST. GUILLAN

It was four o' clock in the a.m.
and you made mistakes, went out
too far, water over your knees, thighs,
eyes—packing tape over your eyes.
With no more instincts left,
everyone had instincts but you.
                    Too exhausted, the fun
had flipped into bewilderment,
into that end-of-the-rope coldness
and derangement in the backseat.
Without a grip, or a hope, or a script
and you'd done all your homework,
at John Jay an honor's student,
smart but regular, and then
there was just you and nobody
but a man and the four wheels
                    he offered you
            that took you
straight into the weeds,
with seeds blowing over you.

CLIFTON WEBB

He seems so imperious and impervious, self-
contained and sharp as a rapier, or a hornet's needle nose.
He is evil reduced to a laser light, as in *Laura*, scanning
the world tightly enough to distill compassion for
itself or, as in *Cheaper by the Dozen*, he is so
level-headed as to be insulting, but always
queer as an eight-legged snake wearing a bow tie.
You were a whole generation, a whole sad
buried generation we will have to excavate.
We'll have to think about. We'll have to know you
and it won't be pretty, but it will make you smile
as you line up all those double scotches
like you did in *Three Coins in a Fountain*
where you played a Maughamish novelist
contemplating dying in Rome, while your secretary
Dorothy McGuire in love with you got drunk,
just like we used to do, to forget.

I WILL ASK MIKE PENCE TO KISS ME

I know it. I know it. That face
blank as the moon excites me,
    makes me feel all hard
inside. He is such an Eagle Scout,
such a serious contender for
the face of crime control.
He looks so grave, so sober,
like Daddy as an undertaker,
that somebody needs to juice him up,
lighten his loafers, make him glow,
make him show a little pulse,
make him show he's got jism
at his fingertips. So,
I will volunteer my time,
just to get Mike off his pedestal,
that one eons lower than his
              former boss,
the one whitewashed in Indiana, the
one presented to him by the American
Legion, the Kiwanis Club, the Rotarians,
and the K. of C. The one
he's glued to by Alien tape. OK
I will unglue him. Undo him
perhaps. Just you wait, Mike.
      Just you wait. *Kiss me!*

STILL IN LOVE WITH LANCE ARMSTRONG

You were the ultimate *goyishe* kid in Paris
with those crystal blue eyes the Greeks jumped
naked in. The dimpled face, the sandy hair,
the creamy skin—and a heart tested at two
and a half times normal human capacity
to beat fatigue, to beat anything. You were
the boy-next-door who stormed the palace,
but had no idea who fathered you.

No, you were created by Mom
who adored you, and you skipped
from woman to woman in a spin
that left you soon unmoored, adrift:
the risk of ex-jocks who one moment
dazzle us, and become only
question marks the next.

Odes should have been written
for you, and shirts designed
to keep your aura alive (like
Lacoste), but instead you
ate crow, and lacked a longer mission,
the *tour*, the life-flowering of yourself:
it stopped just when the words ran out
not the pictures. Lance, buddy,
open your mouth. Say something
so leanly beautiful, so propelled
against the dullness of defeat
and the weary, life-sucking leak
of age that it will push you directly up
into the sky, where you will join
the constellations and the other stars
whose emblazoned faces cheat
fate and are known in a single
comet's swirl of a thought.

Note: Lance later admitted to "doping," and that all of his Olympic victories were basically stolen.

O'SHAE

You were killed barechested at
                at a gas station
in Brooklyn by a kid who didn't
like tall black men dancing
at night, with the light stark

and cutting around them, making
deadly halos out of the silence
surrounding Beyoncé's songs, that
blasted through time that stopped,
                and confronted
an anger that had nothing to do

with your dance.

                But with you, tall
and beautiful, articulate of body,
wise of eye, soft of mouth, long
fingers, wide shoulders, black chest,
                and there you were
with the kid shooting you on his
phone,
            and you stepped up
into that void of hot summertime
while others watched until you
              fell—
stuck, bleeding—and your friend
Otis held you and pressed the blood
with his hand until the ambulance
arrived—and we were all crying,
all of us there, all of us seeing,
your friends and ten siblings
and family and rows and rows
of marching people crying.

Only knowing when you died
at Maimonides Hospital that
a real part of us had known
death too, had felt it deep
            in the rolling rivers
of your life

O'Shae Sibley, murdered the night of July 29, 2023. His friend Otis Pena tried to stop the bleeding with his hand.

THE FORGOTTEN CHILDREN

The forgotten children of Israel
    and Gaza will see trauma
and carnage for the rest of their lives.
They will see it when they sleep and
walk alone or with others, when
        they bathe privately
or with others, when
       they speak with others
or alone to themselves. When they
    seek solace with others,
or solace alone; when they wake
suddenly alone or in the presence of others,
     when others become bodies
wrapped in white shrouds
or black body bags; when others
touch them in anger or genuine
kindness, when others become brothers
revoked of freedom, or sisters taken,
tortured, jailed or broken, burned
in their hair, scared, sobbing,
they will see them. While others
       remain puzzled—
why is time useless? Why do
the same pictures repeat themselves
   with a history that knows no
release or softening aspect,
      except tears—
and oceans of blank regrets?

THE RESTLESS YEARNING SSTOWARDS MY SELF

I see it as I am rowing on the dark waters
towards a rock, large and bright—like
a moon, rigged, distant, rising at the end.
It is that marker, moorage, beckoning;
I dreamed of it in the cold, my body
rolled, amphibian-soft, primitive
as defense. Soon, I will be at its mouth
and its eyes will look down and invite me.
My adventure has been marvelous,
but what good is it without a confidant
to share secrets with at the end?

All destinations are a disappointment
unless you find in them the fulfillment
of a wish. I wanted so perversely
for you to embrace me and be amazed,
like Marco Polo's friends, pelted
with glittering emeralds ripped
from the secret seams of his travel garments.
But you said, exactly as I wanted, "I knew
you were capable, cunning, adventurous,
earnest, and at the end, worthy of my love.
Look what you brought me—

all these treasures! And your own self,
that body, worn, bruised and broken—
feet blistered, fingers splitting,
the behind stiff as an old bony dog's.
Your sweet, impassioned sadness,
all that you've given me, I have listened
and gratefully—gosh!—I accept.
We'll be good jolly buddies
and I'll take your hand and ask you
to leave your boat and sit calmly on my head.
You may kiss my face like I'm both
a monument and a dummy. Its mute
intelligence will accept you, so
your thoughts will ripple out,
denying a single element of despair.
They will comfort you like old prayers

before an operation, when they wheel you
through the hallways and your eyes
straight up at the ceiling
see my face.

"Now tenderly I shall join you
and trace your way, all the way back.
My friend, we've found each other
at last. You worked so hard—all around you
was a vast thing, that big show: choruses,
stars and the hands who nightly hurried
the scenery back and forth—brought on
to make you forget your final place
and destination; but be pleased now,
you've found it, and I will blow
warmth on your brow. You, my bewitching treasure,
will sleep now on my shoulders
and find the dreams you longed for
in the deep curve of my neck."

SEVEN P.M. IN SAN FRANCISCO

It is seven p.m. in San Francisco,
at the corner of Church and Market,
and I am sitting in a fast-food joint
that serves pieces of roast chicken
and despite the grind of sameness
that chases each man away
from the moment, the air seems
to hum with possibilities,
with action, desire, excitement.
And the giddy lights of traffic
are streaming, dream-like, in front of me,
and young men are scurrying
up and down, on the way to this
and that and are thinking about tomorrow,
because it's going to be

so different from today. While fear
for a moment seems to have cleared
the night, early as it is, dropping on us
hope like money in the bank, in the form
of time that we can dance to
and enjoy all the way to Sunday.
It is Saturday night and early,
and we're in this pleasurable city
of streetcars and hills and views;
and the sea way, way out there,
all beckoning and salty and clear—
like the air, does not inspire fear
tonight, but only temptations of delight:
all there in San Francisco
on a warm, early fall Saturday night.

TWA FLIGHT 800

The accounts said it was just a ping,
a pop, and that was the last thing
on the flight recorder in the cockpit
and the question was: was everyone
killed by the explosion or did they drown
after the plane went down
off East Moriches, Long Island;
and we imagine for a moment—something
no one can help—the downspin and the agony
and then the surrender of the sixteen kids
from the Montoursville, Pennsylvania, French club
going to Paris, the boys who must have been ridden
by the other guys for taking French
and the girls who were going to the most
glamorous place in the world, where the magazines
came from—and their parents who had dreamed about this,
saying good-bye, waving; "Just another kiss, come on!"
and who had worked to get the kids on the flight—and Jed Johnson,
the decorator from Greenwich Village and his quiet rooms that looked
like you could just wander into them and sit
and find a moment there all to yourself,
and the newly-wed Italian couple and all the other strangers
who would meet in this most intimate way: and later
be met coldly; clinically; as little pieces
in a puzzle. And the faces that night—
who could not imagine the faces,
the excitement, the jokes, the laughter
and the screams and deep silence
that followed, as each was tossed on a single pop,
a snap in the fingers of time and what
it did to them; and to us.

ALL SELFIES, ALL THE TIME!

We are in Italy and it's all selfies,
all the time. Selfies in Venice,
and selfies in Rome, selfies in
                            Verona
and Padua. Selfies in doubles
and selfies alone, selfies by
                            daylight
and selfies by night. It is infinite
this world of your picture, making
you famous, making you loved,
as long as there are selfie moments
in scores—how we adore them,
these pictures of us. How we abhor
an unselfied rush, anything that
disturbs these pictures of us,

of me, and me, and me alone:
me on that stick, just *me*—but alone.

A WALK THROUGH OLD UDAIPUR

Cows all over the place, and cow dung,
and filthy concrete, grooved with gutters,

scooters dashing in and out,
and people very sweet smiling,
not pushing at you, but opening
hearts to Lord Shiva and his wife Parvati,
for the Lord rides on a bull and the bull
is his messenger: the bull says,
"Fear not, I will bring Shiva's mercy to you."
      You listen for that,
the dust is choking and scooters
shoot past inches from you. Children
with dark opaque eyes watch,
their bare feet steady on the cracked
         sidewalk.

I pass a German café with blondes
sipping coffee, and a small place selling
Mexican food, which seems so far away
in India, but is so close now,
really as everything here is,
even with too much to see
and too much to know. But I will know it,
I will. Just for this instance with Shiva.

CUBA IN THE MORNING

Before daylight; breezes on
palm trees, the lunar silence
of street lamps and stop lights,

saying goodbye to the noise
and *suave* people, to the smiles
and handshakes, the music in cafes,
                the bars and mojitos,
the handsome men and beautiful women,
Moors and Cristianos, flan, and batidos,

in the quiet of thought, of memory,
of going. Of being alive
and knowing, remembering,

finding flowers and big trees
around you telling you we are
grateful for your presence, for all
of life. Life is an island of two
people, or forever or even one.

AS YOU LEAVE THE TRAIN

As you leave the train,
please watch the gap between
the train and the platform,

between the platform and heaven,
between what you can accomplish

and what you desire to happen,
between desire and impulse,
between hopeless blind action
and that singular moment
        of reflection

when you become restored
to humanity again after a weightless
levitation to the spheres

in the wordless gap of tomorrow
that appears now, on the other side.

NEW YORK IS FILLED WITH BOYS

Suddenly New York is filled with boys—
fourteen-year-old boys and sixty-year-old
boys, twelve-year-old boys and forty-year-old
guys—and for a moment they've discarded the
usual Gotham shell and are showing their
boy parts to all the world, which in New York
is New York. They're mad and happy and
kinda crazy all over with the luck of
being boys in New York, eating hot dogs

and pretzels and *not* radicchio, and scrunching
potato chips in their palms to slide down their throats
                         and slurping peaches and mangos
in the streets and spitting stones
at their feet and not thinking about the cops
who are everywhere but not bothering boys
which is only right. Because there are
certain days when New York should be
made out of boys. Only boys.

SIR GAWAIN AT CHRISTMAS

On the feast of Christ, Sir Gawain went out
to balance the scales of honor, seeking
the Green Knight who had claim t' Gawain's
young head, promis'd in return for his own
        beheading at the great hall of Arthur,
though—and lo!—the Knight, magic itself,
had restored his fierce skull, returning it to its
        proper place on his broad shoulders,
but not before claiming an oath on Gawain,
most simple, unadorned, and pure of youth.
And so Sir Gawain had to ride forth
to find the Green thing, a massive monster,
        all same from brow to boots,
so Gawain went forth, in the spirit of goodness,
as blank a creature as goodness claims
itself to be, carrying before him his bright
orb of prayer, a globe of visions imprinted with
dreams, insights, and callings, on which
all folk appeared, all the world in its perfection
and error, faith and doubt, knowing
        and sin, and inside the globe
bathed in purest light, was Jesus himself
    in a glory that forgave all slights
with true kindness and lavished man in his
rawest nature with the sweet gaze of good
even in the rank bitterness of moments.
                    And Jesus

looked on Sir Gawain and Gawain
did not cry out, but only nodded
and offered his young soul to him,
and Jesus also nodded, but would not
take it but disappeared as this sphere
        grew larger and more arraigned
with feats and visages of time, both
           terrible and sublime,
and Gawain watched until it rested
in the bright moonlight of dark winter.
Hares approached and hind, onto a clear meadow

with the moon's face behind and they watched
as Sir Gawain pledged his life and that of
                        his kind
to peace, harmony, and love resigned
to selfless good. Then the reach of the orb
                                burst
        and the moon's white face

fell from sight, but Gawain pressed on
      in the dark and found
the remote castle of the magician
who would turn him from a callow lad
in love with the shield of his own purity
                into a man.

WHITE CHRISTMAS

Only a Jew could have written
"White Christmas," with that huge
yearning for a time that never was
and is not going to be, that perfect
distillation of childhood and memory,
of deep fields of snow, horses, sleigh bells,
and down covers. To come here
                from Polish Russia
to invent yourself as American, to invent
America truly, as I have done
and we all do each day with a difficulty
              slippery with possibilities.
Irving, it's "white Christmas"
here at your fingertips. Close your eyes
and inhale its magic as you played it
            late at night on the black keys
                in New York.

STARLIGHT AT CANAAN

This dance of light from afar
in the heavens, five hundred feet
up in the woods, with shooting stars
and meteorites and comets glowing
leaving paths of crystals burning above,
necks craning, eyes opening
gateways to the heart, so deep, expanding,
                          as far
as the firmament is high, and black.
True black, but etched with constellations
we see now clear as dreams,
such things more magical than art,
more real than eons of fiction—
how did this come back to us,
from so far that mastodons seem
recent and the Ice Age only yesterday;
and yet here we are in the eye's bright
                          wonder
in its perfect acceptance of marvel,
while stars shoot above and leave
their message for each to behold:
this is a thing you cannot keep,
but must know, must accept,
        like the silent paths holy men cut
into the complex schemes of human life.

FOR GREG LOUGANIS

You were adopted and never fit in
but wanted to, inside your young heart;
your dives were a wrinkle on the whole
                            body,
              on art,
on the pleasures of existence, on
the division between air and water,
on the paltry rift between the genders,
on the unbelieving faces and mouths
that hissed at you. They called you
names as a kid, tried to shame you,
hurt you, but you wanted great arms
to hold you, to wrap you in acceptance
and peace, to lift you skyward
against death, like that perfect leap
          like a songbird singing
in space that you did from the board,
that made us gasp. That made
the hollow air define itself
with your body in its twist between
                         the sun
                  and the water.

FOR TWO COPS—
FOR JASON RIVERA, 22,
AND WILBERT MORA, 27

Sometimes one dies in New York
in an instant, violent way,
    or two die at the end of
a long hallway in Harlem,
interceding in a "domestic dispute"
between a son and a mother,
and the mother calls the cops
and the cops come, and they are
                               young
and guided by friendly intentions,
and not wary cynicism, and
their deaths disarm the whole city,
and make long lines of cops weep,
that this sacrifice to the system,
                       twisted
out of recognition, needed to be
made and people "upstairs" swear
to repair it, to change the whole
        mechanics of it, with
the guns and the desperation
and the express route to violence
greased by the spit of poverty
and the hot sear of anger. But

like one of those tragedies the Greeks
            excelled at, only a vast
and emptying nobility can rearrange
the stars and their reckless courses,
can force us to handle such a loss
that we cannot name it
without seeing their faces—
           these two young men,
their smiles, their good feelings
now spread like the evening blue
in January over the city, as it
tries once more to stand up straight.

FOR JACK NICHOLS, 1938-2005, A "GENTLE SOLDIER OF BEAUTY."

You were not known as the gay man of
                    Destiny, but
tapped a courage deeper than Lawrence's truly,
and shared his love for the "Oriental," the
        secretive, the codes; and like him
your life took on doubt and pushed it away
like a faulty raft, with the creamy softness
of your voice and tall body, your classic looks.
But that brain of yours was so honest really,
forthright, fixing steely on lost empires of truth
then moving freely on its own—even murder
could not stop it; and your own many-chambered
mystery marched on, while you watched it,
checking on your boyhood project of revelation,
waiting to talk it, even hold it. I wondered
how you did it, charmed yourself into being,
this gentle soldier of beauty who could shrug off hate
                          then smile—
maybe it was your grandfather who passed you
thoughts from Ingersoll, Whitman, and Burns
and who loved you so deeply, while your dad
a tight-lipped FBI agent stood aside: now
you're swimming in the same Florida pool
all cloud white and heavenly blue, doing laps
with the tiles reflecting your faces,
        and eyes winking back at you.

You were so soft, all silky haired, steady,
Lige-Clarked and leggy, talked slightly
hill-billyish, could smile at anyone even
a tad smart, could make us laugh so,
had such a story to tell, about leaving home
but finding yourself and never for a moment
feeling bad if you knew where the heart's truth
                          stays,
a thing hidden for hundreds of years, but now
                Jack has his say.

PATRICK KENNEDY LEAVES

After living for thirty-two years down below,
Patrick Kennedy, our super, is going
to leave us. We will miss his wry
Irish humor and constant courtesies,
the way he guarded our paths
and walkways from the indignities
of dog urine and casual stupidity
and how he rose up before the sun
on snowy mornings, shoveling us out
with bravery and an iron will, despite
the freezing cold and a runny nose,
and headaches from the work, and
a back that wanted normal rest.

We will miss that he was the
uncommon denominator of
our stories, our times here, just
and unjust, that he suffered with us
and sometimes suffered us,
that he knows all the secrets of
the buildings and many of our own,
that he was the guardian of many
discretions and a patient witness
to our difficulties with the City
and the trials of New York, and a man
who stood among us, steadily watching
the tides of life and real estate
bring others to us, and carry others
away, so as a witness and a provider
of solace in the temporary struggle
of our time here, he was without
equal, and we will miss him sorely.
We will.

THE DEATH OF ISAAC

I just learned today, the one
    after Rosh Hashanah,
of the death of Isaac, the man
who cut my hair for twenty years,
a Russian Jew from Kazakhstan,
who lived near Coney Island
with his wife and four kids,
who always gave me the most
wonderful haircuts, neat and
beautiful with just the right amount
of flourish, who was interested
in my story and had a one-man shop
in the Village, and who once asked me
"When did you first know you were
                        a gay boy?"
and I said, "About twelve, but
you don't know it. You just hide
                  it."
He's dead. Suddenly. Too much
work, six days a week. Too much
standing and cutting, and worrying
about the rent and his kids,
and parking the car, and driving in
from Brooklyn, and trying to make
sense out of dollars. He told me
he'd been a barber in Russia;
he'd always been a barber.
It was a very Jewish profession
there, in that real world he'd left
and the less real one he'd come to.
                I'd
love to think he'd just crossed
over the bar, and is waiting there
for me, with his scissors and smile
and he'd say, "Hello, buddy.
The usual?" And I'd say, "Yes,"
when the time came as it

always does to have your hair cut.
Even when the time stops—
      there's that moment to
have your hair cut—when the
gray light comes and shines
in the softness of dreams with
    Isaac waiting, across the bar.

FAME

The call back that didn't come,
the audition that got cancelled,
the movie whose producer died,
and the money folded—the promises,
the bewitchment, the giddy, dizzying
                height that feels
        like intoxication and ends
                in vomit at 2 AM,
when the real feel of it ends

and you know it's all been
            snatched from you,
gone like a phantom limb
that you claimed—craved!—
in your brain that knew it, even
        called it by your own name.

It slipped away, into a crevice
colder than the end of a dream,
where all the other dead demigods
go and America's landscape
gleams eternally fresh, all
            Norman Rockwell on you.
There the genuine dummies reign,
those who know fame and how
                    it works,
those who hold on to its whip-sharp
            reins, those whose eyes
        are wide enough to see
death on both sides, and in the middle
a place for me to disappear in rest.

FOR EJAY WEISS

What you really wanted was
a refuge, a mountain to climb
with a refuge on the other side,
a refuge with windows to see
your world. It was art always;
oranges and apples, shells of
sea creatures and the shells
of the World Trade Center, you saw
them from within to look out,
as you saw them from the outside
to penetrate yourself. You had
dimension, you saw dimension,
you glimpsed Einstein, Picasso,
                    Van Gogh
like they were waiting for you,
like you could talk to them,
like a friend who understands
greatness on a human scale.
You will leave the world more
than you ever found here—that
is your magic, your own science—
and sign each page of your own
                    guest book
with your eyes and all the words
you used to paint with now translated
into a map outstretched finally,
                    infinitely,
to the galaxies.

THE LAST WEDNESDAY IN AUGUST

It's the last Wednesday in August and I'm
on the beach with my friend Branden Wallace,
watching him, Eakins-bare-assed, by the receding tide.
He brings seashells and driftwood into flotsamy
dream formations, pointing out directions
in a mindful but fleeting way. The distant hook
of New Jersey. Staten Island. Airports. Riis Park
to the left of us. Seagulls soar and horseshoe crabs
belch in big wriggles below. He kneels
and looks at the magnificence of each change
in his creation, gets up for perspective,
observing the chance materials that
figure the lines. We return
to the waves, chickenfighting with guys
on our shoulders. They capsize, limbs
flinging volleys of brine into the air; soon
we'll be gone and fall will bleach its stern
                                      message
                              into the sand.
            We stretch out while the moon

is slowly released over the back dunes. Men
arrive for an evening's private dispersal
of pleasure as the bay trees and beach plums
soak up their presence in a silvery haze. We forget
           about money and the hard call
    of Manhattan,
until gravity forgives us and sighs,
    lifting us to the stars.

GREG BUCKLEY, JR. 21-YEAR-OLD MARINE LANCE CORPORAL, MURDERED INAFGHANISTAN

You died for a lie: that you were
protecting your country. Your
                      beautiful presence
will no longer shimmer among us.
The songs that you loved will dim
their meanings in your absence.
Your friends will swear they will not
forget you, but they will the way
the war dead are forgotten as the
                    living go on,
pacing in their everyday life,
fretting about the price of gas,
the price of boredom and of poverty,
while you will be this mystery,
this vacuum borne by your parents
on a raft of dreams and tears,
                  and moments
of such weakness that their faces
will be unwilling even to enter sleep,
to find shelter in the distance we run from
a gun pointed at history, like the weapon
                that took you away,
   fired by someone whose face
you knew.

Lance Corporal Greg Buckley, Jr, was one of three Marines killed by an Afghan police officer at a military base in the Helmand Province. The Pentagon reported that the three men were killed while exercising. Buckley was scheduled to go home to Oceanside, Long Island, for a visit only a few days after he was killed.

THE STRANGE, SHY MELANCHOLY OF LA ROTONDA

    It sits in the distance, wrapped
in a forgetful fog. Who owned it,
when? It is this far perfection
of a symmetry that reaches a
Platonic levitation, as if with
little effort, it would rise very
slowly into the mathematics
of heaven and from there read
your dreams, and tell you hope
is never lost as long as you
can conceive of its statuary
                        as real.
It is a blissful fake, and crisp
as white Italian sheets fresh
        from a hotel laundry,
as spumanti and prosecco
and the ringing consonants
of an Italian aria, one whose
vowels have already emptied
your heart of all available
                        feelings,
and the ones left are too private
to expose to anyone but this villa
in the distance that only gets
closer: the distance of great time
that is never ended by death
but only by dullness and boredom,
and that apathy that crushes
                      art;
this cannot be allowed. It is painful.

You approach up the gravel walkway,
past the stables now a place for
                              tourists,
then the stairs—then your heart melts
as you see all the way through it
in this perfect pitch of planning
that brings a distant space directly
to you: the space of gone tomorrows,

and gone yesterdays
that gathers before you in a strange
reality of time here. Time now.

THE ANGELS

I can see them waiting.
They talk to me, hold me
in their arms that shine
like light, Tom with his pale
almost pink hair, his skin
ghost-white, so the blue veins
shown—and Jeff my tall friend
who declared his love for me
immediately, and others
we need others; others who
                come and give us
the kindness of their presence
in a fearful world, a world of
destructive mothers or fathers
who freeze their hearts against
            their own evil.

                  They appear
and thank us for being a part of
their way over, for being an anchor
                  to the world,
and we smile and feel so bright,
like sunlight against the darkness
                of the moon.
We talk quietly, sometimes
without words, and sometimes
with them. Tom holds me
and I feel his naked body near me,
naked after so much pain in living,
and joy, he is now joy, and Jeff
smiles like he wishes he was smoking
a cigarette and talking, telling me
everything about himself, how
he'd been busted for pot in North Carolina
    and spent seven years in jail, where
he'd learned to accept everyone
because they all had their own struggles,
                    and Tom and I

talk about his growing up in Ohio,
where he was the popular boy
with a secret and so much shame,
and then he came to New York
and joined the Gay Liberation Front,
where he walked over to me,
                and told me that
his heart had gone over to me,
he was "grooving" on me, and I
        smiled and kissed him,
and that is the way things come:
simply without defense or barriers,
            in our own guarded life,
without the grip of time, or fear
of death—that wished-for thing
that death will disappear, but
                there is an eternity
in a space we must allow ourselves
to see, and these two are in it, with
the others, irrational as it is. Past
        any legality, and the idiocy
of things that keep them from us,
            and they offer us such
needed rest, that place so
           natural no feeling
is hurt in its moment, because
we know in our eyes and heart
this glow and perfect flowing
        of love.

WHAT WE DID NOT KNOW

That we would pay for the foolish
greed of others with our destiny, our
own children. That we could fail
the rich gifts given us by the earth,
the seasons, the mysteries
of life uncoiling by themselves,
and not see their messengers
sent by the winds, the seas, the land

in gripping pain. That we would ache
for things we could not have
but know them only in the courage
of wise people. What we did not know

was so small we could hold it
in our hands
and bring it to our hearts: the meaning of closeness
and of truth.

THE TRAIN STATION AT SPUYTEN DUYVIL

I was at the train station at Spuyten Duyvil
when the big Amtrak train went across
the little bridge into Inwood
                      that swings out,
and it was mid-September and blue
and cool in the morning, while the gulls in the Hudson
flapped over the small estuary by the bridge.

Then for a moment after the noise of the train,
it was silent and a hollow place was formed
in the city's outer ear, where the human elements
of attraction and denial thin out and there
are still trees and salt in the air. Then I heard

the birds again, lifting themselves
above the river's edge, and the cars
zooming along the Henry Hudson Bridge,
arched like a blue finger over the Harlem River;
            then the madness of people oblivious to real life,
always attempting to lock a frame around it,
resumed.

THE POETS DO NOT SING SONGS ANYMORE

The poets do not sing songs anymore—
our voices have been muted,
have been diluted by stupidity
and commerce and do not spring
from us like nightingales
or the tenor cry of larks
on suicidal flights
to bring back morning heat to their wings.
The poets do not sing
this way—natural—open throated.
Fresh, brave, and in love.
They have become duped and sorrowful,
In debt to dull adulthood. We do not sing
like children, or homosexual troubadours
or painted French courtiers
in consort with Apollo
chasing Hyacinth through marsh lands,
chasing love's own separate scream
that settles like violet ribbons
from a distant mountain, slowly spilling
arabesques and ginger curls
of light upon itself: we poets
do not sing of this, and my heart
suffers in its absence.

ADDITIONAL NOTES ABOUT THE POEMS

My poetry is often written about specific feelings on specific dates, so here are most of the "birth" dates of the poems, and some pertinent notes about them.

A Life Without Money, July 23, 2010, Bronx, NY.

New York is full of a million pictures, Sept. 29, 2015, Bryant Park.

Let me be grateful, November 3, 2020 (Election Day) Bronx, New York.

The Lord of Lost Things, January 25, 2016, MOMA, Picasso Sculpture show.

For the Rodriguez Twins, August 2, 2019, New York, NY

Cnidarian, Dec. 14, 2003, Bronx. Cnidarian (C is silent) pertaining to the invertibrate phylum Cnidaria: jellyfish, hydras, sea anemones, and corals.

The Lord of the Lonely, New York, June 2, 2021.

E*nlightenment: March 22, 1999,* Mar. 22, 1999. (New York: in front of the Grace Building, where I am sitting on a balustrade.)

Infinite Starlight, May 1, 2018, Bronx, NY.

For Two Teenage Boys Hanged in Iran for Homosexual Offenses, July 30, 2005. On July 19, two teens, whom some gay activists have felt were probably gay, were murdered in Mashad in northeastern Iran. They were Mahmoud Asgari and Ayaz Marhoni, 18 and 19-year-old boys, and they were murdered by state hanging by Iran's theocratic dictatorship, after a show trial, for allegedly "raping" a 13-year-old boy, and also for drinking alcohol. Human Rights Watch had been monitoring the trial, and protested this inhumanity. According to Shirin Ebadi, an Iranian human rights lawyer and Nobel Prize recipient, 40 other young men and juveniles have been sentenced to death and are awaiting execution in Iran. Many of these young men have been accused of homosexual offenses. This is an outrage against all decency and humanity. For more information on this crime against humanity, see Human Rights Watch accounts.

The Soul Mate, June 12, 2021, train into New York.

The Death of the Peonies, June 3, 1999 Bronx, New York. For Hugh on his birthday, June 30, 1999

OK, So I Met James Franco, Dec. 4, 2011, train into New York.

I Can Not Believe It, August 14, 1999

A Lullaby for the Earth, Mar. 6, 2007, Bronx, NY.

The "Four Last Songs" at Ikea, Sept. 1, 2008, Labor Day, at Ikea in Red Hook, Brooklyn.

Death Awakening, March 20, 2013, New York, NY.

Visages, Nov. 28, 2009, train into New York, before trip to Philadelphia.

The Island of Boyhood, May 17, 2008.

The train emerges, Oct. 4, 2006.

Maserati, July 16, 2014, New York, NY.

A Eulogy for Bernard Madoff, March 11, 2009, Bronx, NY.

Immette St. Guillan, March 15, 2006, train into New York. Immette St. Guillan was a young John Jay student murdered after leaving a bar at last call in the financial district.

Clifton Webb, Dec. 13, 2010, at Co-op City, the Bronx.

I Will Ask Mike Pence to Kiss Me, August 2, 2023.

Still in Love with Lance Armstrong, May 28, 2007, Bronx, NY.

O'Shae, August 2, 2023, Bronx, NY , 12:30 AM,

The Forgotten Children, Nov. 24, 2023, for James Teschner, Bronx, NY.

The Restless Yearning Towards My Self, November 30, 1999, Bronx, NY

Seven P.M. in San Francisco, Nov. 8, 1997.

TWA Flight 800, July 26, 1996, Bronx, New York.

All Selfies, All the Time!, Nov. 4, 2016, Florence, Italy.

A walk through old Udaipur, Feb 22, 2018, Udaipur, India.

Cuba in the morning, Feb 19, 2016, before leaving Havana, 5 AM.

As you leave the train, Dec 1, 2007, 1 Train into New York, for Hugh Young.

New York Is Filled with Boys, August 21, 2013, in Bryant Park, for Ricardo Limon.

Sir Gawain at Christmas, December 15, 2010.

White Christmas, Dec. 18, 2009, Bronx, NY, for John Wallowitch

Starlight at Canaan, July 22, 2012, Canaan, NY, for Barry Safran and Steven F. Dansky.

For Greg Louganis, April 13, 2021, New York, NY

For Two Cops—For Jason Rivera, 22, and Wilbert Mora, 27, January 25, 2022, Bronx, NY

For Jack Nichols, 1938-2005, a "gentle soldier of beauty." May 5, 2005, Bronx, NY. Note: Robert Ingersoll, American orator and proponent of free thinking. Lige Clark was Jack's lover, murdered by bandits in Mexico in 1975

Patrick Kennedy Leaves, March 11, 2014, Villa Charlotte Bronte, Bronx, NY

The death of Isaac, Monday, Sept. 21, 2020, Bronx, NY. For Isaac Sadikov 1970-2020,

Fame, August 23, 2015 (for Candis Cayne, transgender actress)

For Ejay Weiss, June 6, 2018. Ejay Weiss (1942-2018) was a painter and my friend. We became friends later in his life, four years before he died, but realized that we had known each other distantly in New York as young men, in the 1970s.

The Last Wednesday in August, August 26, 2009. Ft. Tilden, Queens, New York

Greg Buckley, Jr. 21-Year-Old Marine Lance Corporal, Murdered in Afghanistan. August 19, 2012, Bronx, New York

The Strange, Shy Melancholy of La Rotonda, Nov. 2, 2016, Vicenza, Italy

The Angels, February 7, 2024. Bronx, NY. For George Thomas Finley and Jeffrey Lann Campbell

What We Did Not Know, Dec. 30, 2012, Bronx, NY.

The Train Station at Spuyten Duyvil, Sept. 19, 1999, Bronx, New York.

The Poets Do Not Sing Songs Anymore, Nov. 8, 1997

PERRY BRASS

Originally from Savannah, Georgia, Perry Brass has published 22 books, including poetry, novels, short fiction, science fiction, and advice books (*How to Survive Your Own Gay Life; The Manly Art of Seduction; The Manly Pursuit of Desire and Love*). A member of the New York Gay Liberation Front, he has been involved with lgbtq rights since 1969, shortly after the Stonewall Uprising, co-editing *Come Out!*, GLF's groundbreaking newspaper. In 1972, with two friends, he co-founded the Gay Men's Health Project Clinic, the first clinic specifically for gay men on the East Coast, still thriving as the Callen-Lorde Community Health Service. His often extremely lyrical poetry has been frequently set to music by composers like Chris DeBlasio, Christopher Berg, Fred Hersch, Paula Kimper, Ricky Ian Gordon, Mary Carol Warwick, Gerald Busby, and Judith Cloud. His sexually frank novels are visionary: they include *Albert or the Book of Man*, 1995, which prefigured the rise of a "White Christian Party" that would control America, curbing reproductive, gay, and women's rights; *The Harvest*, 1997, about the wholesale use of "harvested" human organs; *The Substance of God, a Spiritual Thriller*, 2004, about the rise of a powerful religious fundamentalist network of business interests; and *Carnal Sacraments*, 2007, about a mega-corporation (Amazon?) that would rule the world. He has also published *A Real Life*, "Like Mark Twain with Drag Queens," a memoir about hitchhiking from home in 1965 at the age of 17 and finding an underground network of queer teens like himself supporting each other. He is available for readings and appearances, and can be reached through his website, www.perrybrass.com or on Facebook.

OTHER BOOKS BY PERRY BRASS

SEX-CHARGE

"... poetry at its highest voltage ..." Marv. Shaw in Bay Area Reporter.
Sex-charge. 76 pages. $6.95. With male photos by Joe Ziolkowski. ISBN 0-9627123-0-2

MIRAGE

electrifying science fiction

A gay science fiction classic! An original "coming out" and coming-of-age saga, set in a distant place where gay sexuality and romance is a norm, but with a life-or-death price on it. On the tribal planet Ki, two men have been promised to each other for a lifetime. But a savage attack and a blood-chilling murder break this promise and force them to seek another world, where imbalance and lies form Reality. This is the planet known as Earth, a world they will use and escape. Finalist, 1991 Lambda Literary Award for Gay Men's Science Fiction/Fantasy. This classic work of gay science fiction fantasy is now available in its new Tenth Anniversary Edition.

"Intelligent and intriguing." Bob Satuloff in New York Native.
Mirage, Tenth Anniversary Edition. 230 pages. $12.95. ISBN 1-892149-02-8

CIRCLES

the amazing sequel to Mirage

"The world Brass has created with Mirage and its sequel rivals, in complexity and wonder, such greats as C. S. Lewis and Ursula LeGuin." Mandate Magazine, New York.
Circles. 224 pages. $11.95. ISBN 0-9627123-3-7

OUT THERE

Stories of Private Desires. Horror. And the Afterlife.

"... we have come to associate [horror] with slick and trashy chiller-thrillers. Perry Brass is neither. He writes very well in an elegant and easy prose that carries the reader forward pleasurably. I found this selection to be excellent." The Gay Review, Canada.
Out There. 196 pages. $10.95. ISBN 0-9627123-4-5

ALBERT

or The Book of Man

Third in the Mirage trilogy. In 2025 the White Christian Party has taken over America. Albert, son of Enkidu and Greeland, must find the male Earth mate who will claim his heart and allow him to return to leadership on Ki. "Brass gives us a book where lesser writers would have only a premise." Men's Style, New York.

"If you take away the plot, it has political underpinnings that are chillingly true. Brass has a genius for the future." Science Fiction Galaxies, Columbus, OH.

"Erotic suspense and action . . . a pleasurable read." Screaming Hyena Review, Melbourne, Australia.

Albert. 210 pages. $11.95. ISBN 0-9627123-5-3

WORKS
and Other 'Smoky George' Stories, Expanded Edition

"Classic Brass," these stories—many set in the long-gone seventies, when, as the author says, "Gay men cruised more and networked less"—have recharged gay erotica. This Expanded Edition contains a selection of Brass's steamy poems, as well as his essay "Maybe We Should Keep the 'Porn' in Pornography."

*Work*s. 184 pages. $9.95. ISBN 0-9627123-6-1

THE HARVEST
a "science/politico" novel

From today's headlines predicting human cloning comes the emergence of "vaccos"—living "corporate cadavers"—raised to be sources of human organ and tissue transplants. One exceptional vacco will escape. His survival will depend upon Chris Turner, a sexual renegade who will love him and kill to keep him alive.

"One of the Ten Best Books of 1997," Lavender Magazine, Minneapolis.

"In George Nader's Chrome, the hero dared to fall in love with a robot. In The Harvest—a vastly superior novel, Chris Turner falls in love with a vacco, Hart256043." Jesse Monteagudo, The Weekly News, Miami, Florida.

Finalist, 1997 Lambda Literary Award, Gay and Lesbian Science Fiction.

The Harvest. 216 pages. $11.95. ISBN 0-9627123-7-X

THE LOVER OF MY SOUL
A Search for Ecstasy and Wisdom

Brass's first book of poetry since Sex-charge is worth the wait. Flagrantly erotic and just plain flagrant—with poems like "I Shoot the Sonovabitch Who Fires Me," "Sucking Dick Instead of Kissing," and the notorious "MTV Ab(solutely) Vac(uous) Awards, The Lover of My Soul again proves Brass's feeling that poetry must tell, astonish, and delight.

"An amazingly powerful book of poetry and prose," The Loving

Brotherhood, Plainfield, NJ.
The Lover of My Soul. 100 pages. $8.95. ISBN 0-9627123-8-8

HOW TO SURVIVE YOUR OWN GAY LIFE
An Adult Guide to Love, Sex, and Relationships

The book for adult gay men. About sex and love, and coming out of repression; about surviving homophobic violence; about your place in a community, a relationship, and a culture. About the important psychic "gay work" and the gay tribe. About dealing with conflicts and crises, personal, professional, and financial. And, finally, about being more alive, happier, and stronger.

"This book packs a wallop of wisdom!" Morris Kight, founder, Los Angeles Gay & Lesbian Services Center. Finalist, 1999 Lambda Literary Award in Gay and Lesbian Religion and Spirituality.
How to Survive Your Own Gay Life. 224 pages. $11.95. ISBN 0-9627123-9-6

ANGEL LUST
An Erotic Novel of Time Travel

Tommy Angelo and Bert Knight are in a long-term relationship. Very long—close to a millennium. Tommy and Bert are angels, but different. No wings. Sexually free. Tommy was once Thomas Jebson, a teen serf in the violent England of William the Conqueror. One evening he met a handsome knight who promised to love him for all time. Their story introduces us to gay forest men, robber barons, castles, and deep woodlands. Also, to a modern sexual underground where "gay" and "straight" mean little. To Brooklyn factory men. Street machos. New York real estate sharks. And the kind of lush erotic encounters for which Perry Brass is famous. Finalist, 2000 Lambda Literary Award, Gay and Lesbian Science Fiction.

"Brass's ability to go from seedy gay bars in New York to 11th century castles is a testament to his skill as a writer." Gay & Lesbian Review.
Angel Lust. 224 pages. $12.95. ISBN 1-892149-00-1

WARLOCK
A Novel of Possession

Allen Barrow, a shy bank clerk, dresses out of discount stores and has a small penis that embarrasses him. One night at a bathhouse he meets Destry Powars—commanding, vulgar, seductive, successful—who pulls Allen into his orbit and won't let go. Destry lives in a closed, moneyed world that Allen can only glimpse through the pages of tabloids. From generations of drifters, Powars has been chosen to learn a secret language based on force, deception, and nerve. But who chose him—and what does he really want from Allen? What are Mr. Powars's dark powers? These are the mysteries that Allen will uncover in *Warlock*, a novel that is as paralyzing in its suspense as it is voluptuously erotic. *Warlock*. 226 pages. $12.95. ISBN 1-892149-03-6

THE SUBSTANCE OF GOD
A Spiritual Thriller

What would you do with the Substance of God, a self-regenerating material originating from Creation? The Substance can bring the dead back to life, but has a "mind" of its own. Dr. Leonard Miller, a gay bio-researcher secretly addicted to "kinky" sex, learned this after he was found mysteriously murdered in his laboratory while working alone on the Substance. Once brought back to life, Miller must find out who infiltrated his lab to kill him, how long will he have to live—and, exactly, where does life end and any Hereafter begin?

Miller's story takes him from the underground sex scenes of New York to the all-male baths of Istanbul. It will deal with the longing for God in a techno-driven world; with the persistent attractions of religious fundamentalism; and with the fundamentals of "outsider" sexuality as both spiritual ritual and cosmic release. And Miller, the unbelieving scientist, will be driven himself to ask one more question: Is our often-censored urge toward sex and our great, undeniable urge toward a union with God . . . the same urge?

"Perry Brass has added to the annals of gay lit." -Book Marks.
The Substance of God. 232 pages. $13.95. ISBN: 1-892149-04-4

THE MANLY ART OF SEDUCTION
How to Meet, Talk to, and Become Intimate with Anyone
Winner Gold Medal Ippy Award from Independent Publisher, Gay and Lesbian Non-Fiction. "Men are not supposed to be seductive." Perry Brass proves this is not true. Always waiting for someone else to make the first move, traumatized by your fear of rejection and don't have a clue how to open a conversation or expand the terms of a relationship, then The Manly Art of Seduction is a must-have. Brass explains male territorialism, and how it keeps men locked inside themselves. He talks about making decisions yourself, and how these decisions can be used to make seduction possible—even easy. He deals with rejection, and how to use mind pictures and exercises to rejection-proof your psyche. At the end each chapter are

A LIFE WITHOUT MONEY AND OTHER POEMS

questions you can use to tailor this book to your needs, seeing your own progress as you come to master this art.
"Relationships between men can run the gamut from brief connections to long-lasting commitments. This book demonstrates how to break through fear and old patterns to increase your seduction skills and decrease missed opportunities. No matter what kind of connection you might be looking for, the advice offered here is helpful, sharp, and pulls no punches. But the tough love is served with style and humor."
Dave Singleton, author of The Mandates: 25 Real Rules for Successful Gay Dating
"A first-class primer for every taste," Richard Labonte, BookMarks, nationally syndicated column about glbt books.
"Filled with useful, practical advice, Brass also explores deeper concepts like valor and territorialism, and his stunning chapter on rejection should be a must-read for everyone in the dating scene." Elizabeth Millard, ForeWord Reviews, Jan., 2010.
"What Brass does so well is guide a man in how to get from the initial meeting all the way to the first date and beyond. But the brilliance of the book is that you can actually read it from the perspective of the person being seduced. The "seductee" can see just how open and vulnerable the person approaching them is being, and also see what types of responses they might end up getting back. The seductee might then see himself and begin to understand how his behavior might be affecting the situation. And in that, he might learn how to let down his own guard, and allow that connection to take place."
Kevin Taft, Edge Magazine: Boston. March 1, 2010
The Manly Art of Seduction, 200 pages, $16.95, ISBN: 978-1-892149-06-0
Ebook ISBN: 978-1-892149-10-7

KING OF ANGELS
A Novel About the Genesis of Identity and Belief
    Set in the haunting, enchanting landscape of Savannah, Georgia (*Midnight in the Garden of Good and Evil*), during the tumultuous early 1960s (the Mad Men era), *King of Angels* differs greatly from most novels with an lgbt theme: it is about a significant and extremely compelling relationship between a father and son—told from the bond that both

father and son feel, despite differences in generation, the many secrets that separate them, and barriers of temperament but not of basic character. This nourishing father-and-son relationship is something many gay men (as well as straight men) seek, but it has been sadly missing, and missed, from most literature.

King of Angels explores this bond as part of a re-examination of the male gender and role. As Benjamin Rothberg, the half-Jewish, 12-year-old protagonist of *King of Angels* says about Robby Rothberg, his very tragic but heroic Jewish father, he was the "closest thing to a brother I'd ever have, even though I didn't know it then."
Finalist, Ferro-Grumley Award for Gay and Lesbian Fiction, winner Bronze Medal IPPY
Award for Best Young Adult Fiction. 2012.
King of Angels, ISBN: 978-1-892149-14-5, $18.00 370 pages

THE MANLY PURSUIT OF DESIRE AND LOVE
Your Guide to Life, Happiness, and Emotional and Sexual Fulfillment In a Closed-Down World
If you are what you eat, then why aren't you what you desire? Desire stands in the great no-man's land of human activity: the zone of most conflict, fear, and anxiety. It scares us. We are often asked to hate it—by those who claim to have given it up for "better" things, and who often hypocritically haven't. Their biggest desire is power, and desire, whether you are for it or against it, is a blast furnace of power. Your desires are an opening to the world of your imagination, real feelings, and your larger Deeper Self, the Self that contains that core of your own regeneration we call the "soul." This book, a companion to Brass's *The Manly Art of Seduction*, is a guidebook to exploring and using your own desires without shame, but also with responsibility and maturity. This is a book about "grown-up" sex and "grown-up" feelings in an often infantile world.
The Manly Pursuit of Desire and Love, 240 pages, $16.95, ISBN: 978-1-892149-06-0

A REAL LIFE
Like Mark Twain with Drag Queens
A Memoir. June, 1965. After a year of intimidation and persecution at the University of Georgia in Athens, 17-year-old Perry Brass hitchhiked from his native Savannah to San Francisco, beginning an adventure he called, "like Mark Twain with drag queens." Often dead broke, he met an underground of homeless gay kids like himself, boy hustlers and the men who frequented them, as well as tormented married men, female impersonators, and ruthless cops.
A Real Life is a keyhole into being an openly gay teen in the closeted period before Stonewall, and Gay Liberation. Brass also gives an account of his abusive lesbian mother, the many jobs and "hustles" he pursued to stay alive, the beautiful teenage hustler he fell hopelessly in love with, and the older men who taught him how to live in the shadowy gay world.
"A Real Life, 'Like Mark Twain with Drag Queens," 223 pages, paperback, $16.95. ISBN:978-1-892149-29-9

TRIAL BY NIGHT,
Two Novellas of Gay Love, Horror, Innocence, and Deception
If you have ever been in love way over your head, this is the book for you. In TRIAL BY NIGHT, Perry Brass, author of bestselling classics like *Angel Lust, How to Survive Your Own Gay Life,* and *The Manly Art of Seduction*, presents two novellas, longer short fiction, exploring love, the innocence of falling in love, and deception, that snake in the garden path. In the first, *Ghosts or The Dangerous Fog*, he presents himself as a fictional character and meets Stephen Hong-Moore, recently divorced from his Chinese husband of many years, and raring to be "gay, single, and in New York." He comes on to Perry like Al Capone at a bootleggers' convention, sweeping Perry into that "dangerous fog" of love, with a potentially lethal undertow in it, the fact that Hong-Moore is "neuro-divergent" and any involvement with him will be measured, guarded, and, most probably, disastrous.
In the second novella, *The Seduction of Perry*, Brass takes us back to the 1990s, and gay Chicago, to a bathhouse assignation with Adam, a young man who so radiates beauty and youthful innocence that anyone will be charmed and struck by him. But his innocence is merely another variation on not

judging any book by its cover—for Adam has secrets of his own, and a lifetime that goes back many, many years beyond his young looks, and that includes the threat of the worst kind of slavery.

    Both of these novellas are tributes to the life of the mind, of books, and of writing—that writers live in places inside themselves that other people want to visit, but that does not safeguard writers, or anyone else, from the dangers around them. These are two novellas of the horror of the human heart. They also deal with autism as well as other places "on the spectrum" that, of course, includes heartbreak.

Trial by Night, Two Novellas of Gay Love, Horror, Innocence, and Deception, 86 pages, $14.95. ISBN: 978-1-892149-35-0

At your bookstore, or from:
Belhue Press
2501 Palisade Avenue, Suite A1
Bronx, NY 10463

E-mail: belhuepress@earthlink.net

Please add $3.00 shipping for the first book and $1.00 for each book thereafter. New York State residents please add 8.25% sales tax. Foreign orders in U.S. currency only.

You can now order Perry Brass's exciting books online at http://www.perrybrass.com. Please visit this website for more details, regular updates, and news of future events and books.

www.ingramcontent.com/pod-product-compliance
Lightning Source LLC
Chambersburg PA
CBHW030100100526
44591CB00008B/216